HAL•LEONARD
INSTRUMENTAL PLAY-ALONG

Audio ACCESS INCLUDED

PLAYBACK+
Speed • Pitch • Balance • Loop

VIOLIN

Disney MARY POPPINS RETURNS

MUSIC BY MARC SHAIMAN
LYRICS BY SCOTT WITTMAN AND MARC SHAIMAN

Can You Imagine That? 2

A Conversation 4

A Cover Is Not the Book.................................5

(Underneath the) Lovely London Sky...............6

Nowhere to Go But Up 8

The Place Where Lost Things Go 10

The Royal Doulton Music Hall 11

Trip a Little Light Fantastic 12

Turning Turtle 14

Audio Arrangements by Peter Deneff

To access audio, visit:
www.halleonard.com/mylibrary

Enter Code
5024-4634-2069-9739

ISBN 978-1-5400-4592-8

HAL•LEONARD®

Visit Hal Leonard Online at
www.halleonard.com

Contact us:
Hal Leonard
7777 West Bluemound Road
Milwaukee, WI 53213
Email: info@halleonard.com

In Europe, contact:
Hal Leonard Europe Limited
42 Wigmore Street
Marylebone, London, W1U 2RN
Email: info@halleonardeurope.com

In Australia, contact:
Hal Leonard Australia Pty. Ltd.
4 Lentara Court
Cheltenham, Victoria, 3192 Australia
Email: info@halleonard.com.au

CAN YOU IMAGINE THAT?

VIOLIN

Music by MARC SHAIMAN
Lyrics by SCOTT WITTMAN and MARC SHAIMAN

A CONVERSATION

VIOLIN

Music by MARC SHAIMAN
Lyrics by SCOTT WITTMAN and MARC SHAIMAN

A COVER IS NOT THE BOOK

VIOLIN

Music by MARC SHAIMAN
Lyrics by SCOTT WITTMAN and MARC SHAIMAN

(Underneath the)
LOVELY LONDON SKY

VIOLIN

Music by MARC SHAIMAN
Lyrics by SCOTT WITTMAN and MARC SHAIMAN

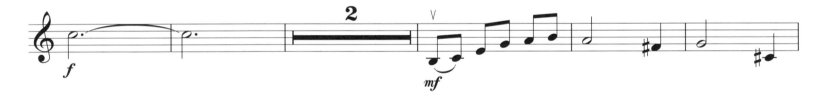

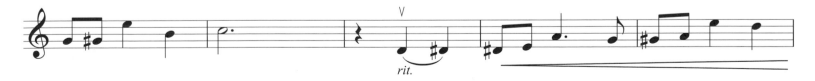

NOWHERE TO GO BUT UP

VIOLIN

Music by MARC SHAIMAN
Lyrics by SCOTT WITTMAN and MARC SHAIMAN

THE PLACE WHERE LOST THINGS GO

VIOLIN

Music by MARC SHAIMAN
Lyrics by SCOTT WITTMAN and MARC SHAIMAN

THE ROYAL DOULTON MUSIC HALL

VIOLIN

Music by MARC SHAIMAN
Lyrics by SCOTT WITTMAN and MARC SHAIMAN

TRIP A LITTLE LIGHT FANTASTIC

VIOLIN

Music by MARC SHAIMAN
Lyrics by SCOTT WITTMAN and MARC SHAIMAN

TURNING TURTLE

VIOLIN

Music by MARC SHAIMAN
Lyrics by SCOTT WITTMAN and MARC SHAIMAN